WINGS
THE CONQUEST OF THE AIR

THE ACES

Christopher Maynard and David Jefferis

Illustrated by
Ron Jobson
and Michael Roffe

Franklin Watts
London   New York   Toronto   Sydney

© 1987 Franklin Watts

First published in 1987 by
Franklin Watts
12a Golden Square
London W1R 4BA

First published in the USA
by Franklin Watts Inc.
387 Park Avenue South
New York, N.Y. 10016

First published in Australia
by Franklin Watts
Australia
14 Mars Road
Lane Cove, NSW 2066

UK ISBN: 0 86313 519 6
US ISBN: 0-531-10367-6
Library of Congress
Catalog Card No: 86-51547

Technical consultant
Tim Callaway, RAF Museum,
Hendon, London

Designed and produced by
Sunrise Books

Printed in Belgium

THE ACES

Contents

Introduction

This book is about the flyers of World War I. During this war Britain, France, Russia, Italy, the United States and other countries were the Allies. Fighting them were Germany, Austria-Hungary, Turkey and Bulgaria, known as the Central Powers.

The battle in western Europe was mainly along a line stretching from the Belgian coast to Switzerland. This was called the Western Front and millions of soldiers died along it during the war which lasted from 1914 to 1918.

The aces were the top pilots of the day, earning the title when they had shot down several enemy planes. The top scorer of the war was the German ace, Manfred von Richthofen. He had 80 victories to his credit before he too was shot down.

In this book, you can read about many ace pilots. There were hundreds of aces though, so there is not room for all of them.

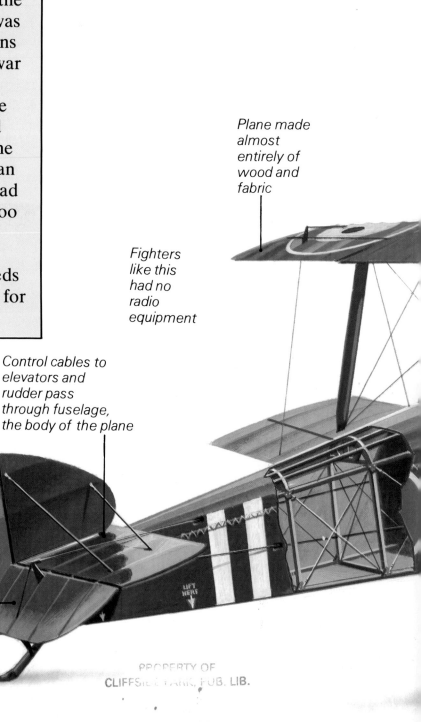

Plane made almost entirely of wood and fabric

Fighters like this had no radio equipment

Control cables to elevators and rudder pass through fuselage, the body of the plane

Rudder used in turns

Elevators pitch the plane up and down

Pilots and planes

The pilots of World War I were mostly in their late teens or early twenties. New pilots arriving at the Front had just a few hours flight training behind them. They had to learn the tactics of air fighting quickly, otherwise they got shot down. Many pilots lost their lives within days of joining their squadron. The great fear of aviators was fire in the aircraft – many pilots were scarred for life or were burnt to death while trapped in the cockpit.

At the beginning of the war, most aircraft were flimsy, extremely unreliable contraptions. By the war's end, military demands had resulted in fast, agile fighters, such as the Camel shown below. Giant bombers could carry heavy loads hundreds of miles to attack enemy targets.

The Sopwith Camel was one of the successful fighters of World War I. It gained more combat victories – 1,294 enemy aircraft in all – than any other plane. The cover over the guns reminded pilots of a camel's hump and this gave the plane its name. In all, 5,490 Camels were built.

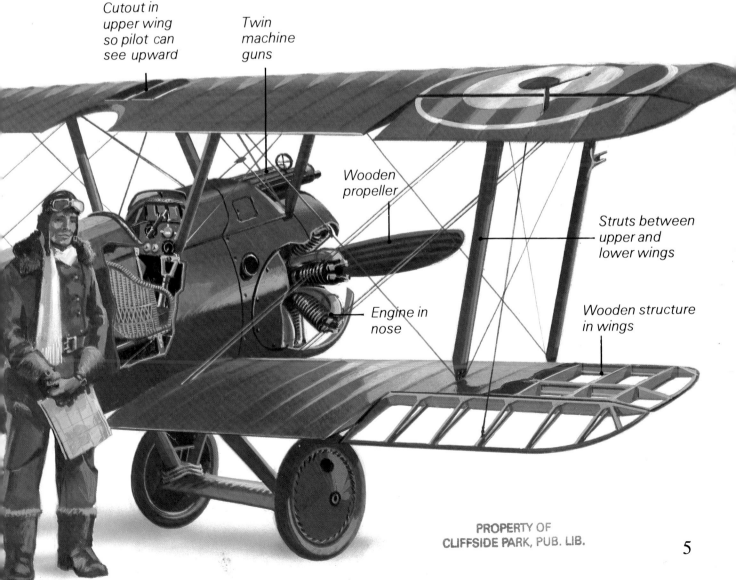

Cutout in upper wing so pilot can see upward

Twin machine guns

Wooden propeller

Engine in nose

Struts between upper and lower wings

Wooden structure in wings

Over the Front

As the fighting in the front lines bogged down in barbed wire and trenches, horse-mounted cavalry proved useless as the traditional "eyes" of the army. Planes quickly took over, though at the start of the fighting, neither side had aircraft that were especially suited to wartime flying.

Even getting to the battle zone could be fairly hair-raising. The pilots of the first British squadron to fly over the English Channel to France in August 1914 all carried inflated bicycle tires as lifebelts – just in case – and were armed only with pistols. Coming in to land at Ostend in Belgium, they were fired on by Royal Marines and French troops who mistook them for enemy aircraft. Soon after, the order went out to paint British flags on the underside of the wings. By December the flags were replaced by colored roundels, a style developed by the French and soon copied by all Allied planes.

Pilots at first were in danger more from their own inexperience than from each other. Their slow, rickety reconnaissance planes had to put up with soldiers taking pot shots at them as they chugged across the lines at speeds of less than 112 km/h (70 mph). The experience of being thrown about by the supersonic shock waves of heavy shells taught pilots to steer clear of artillery fire. In fact, a job for many pilots was "spotting" for artillery gunners. The spotter plane flew near enemy positions relaying the accuracy of the shellfire back to the gunners. One plane returned with a large hole in it where a shell had gone through!

National markings

Dozens of types of aircraft were pressed into service when the war broke out. National markings were not used until it became essential to be able to tell aircraft apart.

In August 1914, a Germany army airship was hit by French ground fire – then it was finished off by German troops. Most troops were inclined to shoot at anything in the sky, including their own aircraft. By the end of November 1914, all the air services had their own markings. These are shown in the pictures below.

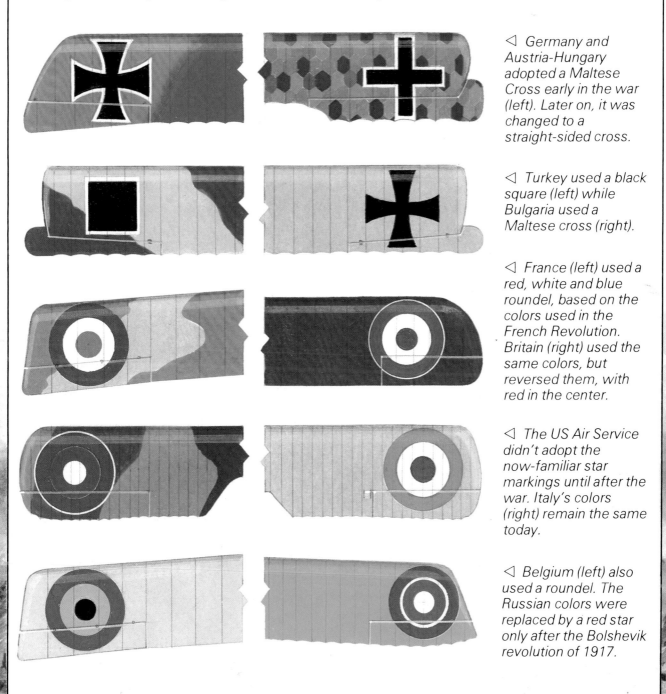

◁ Germany and Austria-Hungary adopted a Maltese Cross early in the war (left). Later on, it was changed to a straight-sided cross.

◁ Turkey used a black square (left) while Bulgaria used a Maltese cross (right).

◁ France (left) used a red, white and blue roundel, based on the colors used in the French Revolution. Britain (right) used the same colors, but reversed them, with red in the center.

◁ The US Air Service didn't adopt the now-familiar star markings until after the war. Italy's colors (right) remain the same today.

◁ Belgium (left) also used a roundel. The Russian colors were replaced by a red star only after the Bolshevik revolution of 1917.

The first dogfight

Although a pilot shooting at another pilot was thought to be ungentlemanly at first, both sides soon forgot this as they tried to stop enemy bombing and reconnaissance flights. The first clash in which one plane shot down another involved a French Voisin LA (Type III) "pusher" biplane and a German Aviatik front-engined "tractor" machine.

On the morning of October 5, 1914, Pilot Joseph Frantz and Louis Quenault, his gunner, of the French Armée de l'Air crossed the Front to bomb troops who were behind Fort Brimont, not far from Reims. On the floor of the plane, they carried six artillery shells, which Quenault dropped over the side onto the enemy. Returning at 2,130 m (7,000 ft), Frantz spotted the two-man Aviatik below him. Using the Voisin's height advantage he dived to lure the German back over French lines.

The German swallowed the bait and gave chase. Both gunners snapped off single shots at every opportunity, with the French airman standing behind his pilot to make the most of his machine gun's wide field of fire. The two planes maneuvered for position, dropping to a mere 180 m (600 ft) in the process. In the trenches, hundreds of troops craned their heads to watch the dogfight overhead.

Quenault, who knew that his heavy Hotchkiss gun was unreliable, only fired single shots. After less than 50 bullets the gun jammed. As he started to clear it, the Aviatik suddenly flipped over, spun down and exploded as it hit the ground. Quenault's last shot had, by chance, killed the pilot. Both German crewmen died, becoming the first victims of air-to-air combat.

▷ In a Voisin, the gunner had to stand up in his seat in order to aim and fire. This was a precarious position since a lurching plane could easily tumble him from his perch.

The Voisin was a "pusher" plane. Its propeller was rear-mounted and pushed the aircraft along. This design was popular in the early days as it left a clear view ahead for gunners to fire.

Tractor designs, with front-mounted props, became more popular as the war progressed.

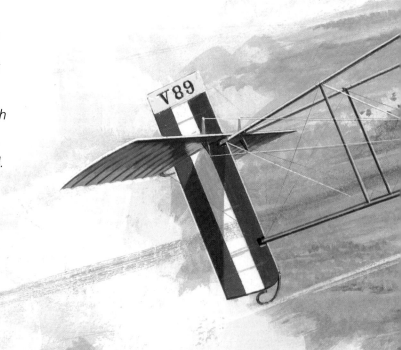

Shooting through propellers

There was no easy way for pilots in planes with front-mounted engines to fire straight ahead, since the spinning propeller was in the path of the bullets. Metal deflector plates could be fitted to the propeller, though bullet shrapnel screaming past a pilot's head hardly encouraged him to press the trigger.

A simple solution to the problem was found in the spring of 1915 by the Dutch designer Anthony Fokker. He built an interrupter gear to control a forward-facing machine gun. It timed the gun so that it only fired between the blades, as the propeller revolved at 1,200 times a minute.

But there were problems with the interrupter gear, as Fokker himself found out. One day, while flying low to test his forward-firing gear, a gun jammed. The plane shuddered in mid-air, then began to shake and vibrate. Fokker just managed a bone-jarring thump of a landing. Having stopped, he climbed out to take a look. He saw that the propeller had taken a direct hit; 16 bullets had embedded themselves in the wood. The unbalanced propeller that had nearly shaken the engine from its mountings was also on the verge of dropping off. If so Fokker would have spun out of control and crashed.

Fokker's escape was lucky. But his problem was not unusual. Quite a few pilots shot their own propellers off – and did this in planes that had no ejector seats or parachutes.

△ Anthony Fokker managed to land his plane safely. Forced landings were not uncommon, though engine failure was the usual reason. One British pilot had to make 22 forced landings in 30 flights!

▷ This diagram illustrates the problem with forward firing guns. The line of bullets passed straight through the propeller disk. The interrupter system connected prop and guns, using a geared arrangement, and the bullets passed between the propeller blades.

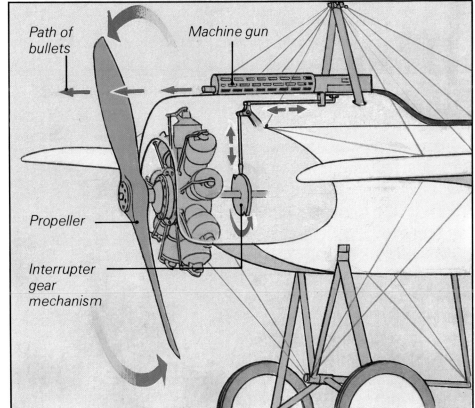

Path of bullets

Machine gun

Propeller

Interrupter gear mechanism

Immelmann's turn

Fokker E.III being chased by an FE2B.

Max Immelmann was one of the first German air aces of the war. In his heyday, between August 1915 and June 1916, he downed 15 planes, becoming known as the "Eagle of Lille," after the area in France where he saw most of his service.

By 1915, fighter pilots learning the ropes of air combat had discovered that the safest way to attack was from above and behind. This angle had the best chance of surprise, especially if you dived out of clouds or with the sun behind you. It also gave you extra speed to close in for a quick kill. But, if you missed your target there was a good chance of overshooting it, and in turn becoming the prey.

Immelmann's solution was to use aerobatic half-loops in combat for the first time. This maneuver became known as the Immelmann Turn. Quite possibly he hit upon the idea after putting his Fokker into a steep climb after a first attack. At the top of it he used the ailerons to roll over and right himself, then dived down onto his opponent a second time – again attacking from behind. Even if the target turned left or right, he could cut to the inside and still hang onto its tail.

△ *Immelmann's Fokker E.III, being chased in a high speed dive by a British FE2B. To escape from the stream of bullets, Immelmann pulls up steeply.*

▷ *He pulls over to start a loop. At the top, he quickly rolls the plane right way up. He has now "turned" through 180°, doing it by a half-loop and half-roll, rather than the usual flat turn.*

Now he has the choice of flying off, turning down to attack from a different angle, or flipping over again and continuing the loop downward. If he does this, as shown, he can get right on the tail of the FE2B.

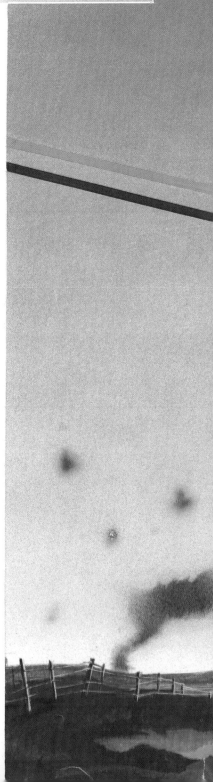

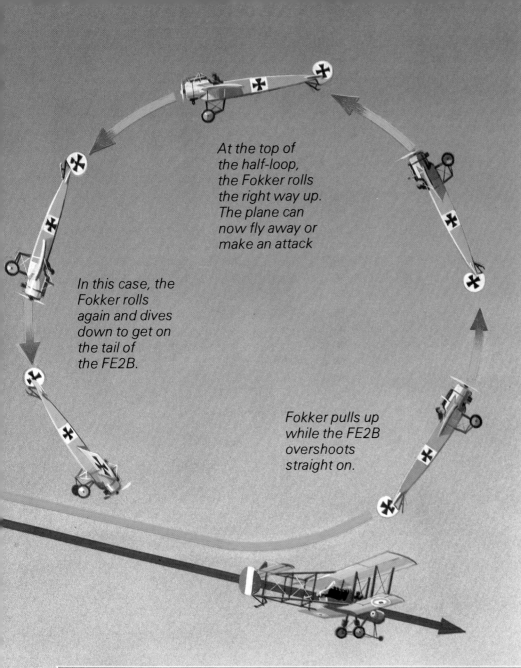

At the top of the half-loop, the Fokker rolls the right way up. The plane can now fly away or make an attack

In this case, the Fokker rolls again and dives down to get on the tail of the FE2B.

Fokker pulls up while the FE2B overshoots straight on.

▽ Immelmann closes the distance until he is less than 100 m (310 ft) away and then opens fire on the FE2B.

It was the British who named the Immelmann turn – Immelmann used it against them over the Front. In fact, several pilots claimed to have invented the "turn" including a Frenchman called Adolphe Pégoud, who was also the first man to loop-the-loop.

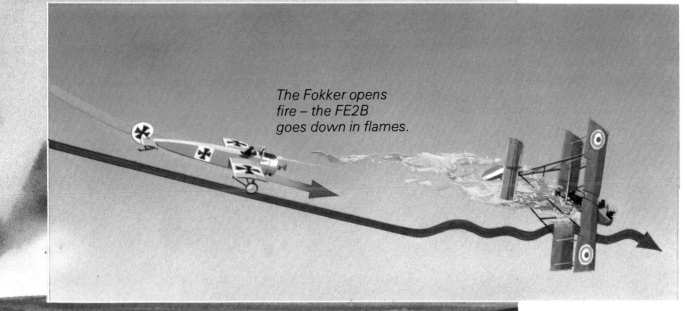

The Fokker opens fire – the FE2B goes down in flames.

13

Bombers

The first successful bombing raid of the war was a German raid on Paris. Four small bombs were dropped on August 30, 1914.

Early bombs were simply loaded into two-seater planes and dropped overboard by the observer. Among the first bombing weapons were flechettes. These were steel darts, about 15 cm (6 in) long. Dropped from the air, they could penetrate soldiers' helmets or anything else in the way. Flechettes or similar weapons had to be perfectly aimed though, so explosive bombs were developed. These did not have to score a direct hit to cause damage. The French used small artillery shells for a while, before proper bombs were made.

By June 1917, Gotha bombers were raiding London. During one raid, in full view of watching crowds below, 14 of the twin-engined German planes circled the city and dropped 72 bombs. 162 people were killed. Not a single bomber was shot down during the raid as the Gothas were able to fly off before any aircraft could climb high enough to attack them. Fighter planes were brought back from the Front to deal with the menace. The Gothas were forced to bomb by night.

△ *Until 1917 Gothas bombed in daylight. But as counter attacks by fighters became more successful the raids switched to the cover of darkness.*

▷ *Antiaircraft defenses were primitive in World War I. Searchlights were used for the first time as were balloons, trailing long wire, designed to cut through aircraft propellers.*

Night fighter units were a late development in the war, and several pilots became skilled at night fighting, including Captain A.B.Yuille who scored six victories. In May 1918, during a single raid, the defending Camels shot down seven Gothas out of a force of 43. After that, the bombing of Britain stopped.

Balloon busting

Tethered observation balloons were widely used by the Germans to keep watch on the opposite front lines. To the unwary, these balloons were fat, tempting targets, being unarmed and unmaneuverable as they bobbed on their thick mooring cables. Yet they were so heavily protected by anti-aircraft guns and patrolling planes overhead that most pilots wisely left them alone. Attacks were simply too hazardous to be undertaken lightly.

A few pilots, however, made balloon busting a private war of their own. One was Frank Luke, an American pilot, who knocked down 14 balloons during September 1918 in a spectacular two week career that ended with his death. During this brief period he became one of the fastest-scoring pilots of the war.

The least dangerous way to attack was a steep dive from above. The pilot passed swiftly through the screen of covering fighters, yet was shielded from the heaviest ground fire by the bulk of the balloon. A high speed dive also made it easier to escape quickly.

On September 18, Luke and his partner, Joe Wehrner, attacked a pair of balloons, dropping from a height of 3,660 m (12,000 ft) so swiftly that neither balloon could be winched down to earth in time. The first exploded as Luke's incendiary ammunition hit the mark. Climbing, he attacked the second one. The balloon's observers (who had parachutes) jumped out of the gondola just before it too burst into flames.

◁ Attacking observation balloons was a risky business and most pilots avoided them.

Frank Luke's usual approach was to swoop down at high speed, past any defending fighters, to make a point-blank attack and a quick escape. The incendiary ammunition used explosive bullets to set fire to the gas-filled balloons.

The Red Baron

The most successful German fighter pilot of the war was Manfred von Richthofen, known by his opponents as the "Red Baron." Between September 1916 and April 1918 he shot down 80 enemy planes, the highest total by any pilot on either side.

Richthofen had an insatiable appetite for combat. His first command, Jasta 11, was staffed with some of the best pilots of the war – the pick of the crop. With a fine touch of psychological warfare he made sure that his enemies all knew about the fearsome fighting crew he led by having his own Albatros painted only scarlet, while the rest of the aircraft in the squadron were painted scarlet and a second color. His gaudy team came to be known as the "flying circus" by Allied pilots who faced it.

Yet for all his skill, luck could still turn against him. Early in July 1917, while his patrol was attacking six planes of the Royal Flying Corps, he was hit and almost killed. During the dogfight, Captain Cunnell and his observer Lieutenant Woodbridge found a red Albatros turning toward them. Woodbridge opened fire at an extreme range of 366 m (1,200 ft) – too far to have much effect – until a lucky bullet clipped Richthofen on the side of the head, knocking him out. He spun out of control, coming to at only 150 m (500 ft). Richthofen made a forced landing and managed to crawl out of the plane before collapsing.

Fighting the cold

Flying in all weather in open cockpits, and at heights up to 7,000 m (20,000 ft), was a terrible strain on pilots. As protection against the bitter cold they bundled up in layers of whatever extra clothing came to hand. Many Allied pilots wore layers of newspaper tucked under their jackets.

Pigskin helmet

Fur-lined, elbow-length mitts

Cut-down leather greatcoat

△ *Winged by a stray bullet, the "Red Baron" made a crash landing before crawling from his plane and collapsing. A few weeks later he was back in the air with his squadron.*

Parachutes were worn only toward the end of the war – and not at all by Allied pilots. The Allied High Command thought that wearing a 'chute would discourage "bold flying" by pilots!

Goatskin boots

Heraldry of the Air

Pilots and crew lived, fought and died in squadron teams. It was a small and close-knit world they shared, which went a long way to keep morale high. Often they adopted a colorful symbol to identify their own unit, and to mark it out from other squadrons in their service. Very often, keen rivalries existed between squadrons to see which one could score most ''kills.''

△ This was the symbol of Rickenbacker's unit, the 94th US Air Squadron.

△ British ace William Barker used a heart and arrow badge on the tail of his maneuverable Sopwith Camel.

△ A prancing horse was used by Italian ace Francesco Baracca. It was later adopted by Ferrari cars.

The racing driver ace

As one of America's leading racing car drivers before the war, Edward Rickenbacker always wanted to fly fast planes. He was in England, racing Sunbeam cars, when America entered the war in 1917. His suggestion to form a fighter squadron made up entirely of racing drivers was ignored by the US Army.

By August 1917, he was in France learning to fly for the US Air Service. But getting into action was a big problem for the Americans, who arrived in France with more pilots than planes. They had to go shopping for whatever machines were available, and it was not until March 1918 that American pilots went into combat. They flew the Nieuport 28, a plane that was not very popular with pilots because of its habit of shedding wing fabric in tight turns or high speed dives.

Rickenbacker was with the very first American patrol over German lines and a month later he shot down his first enemy plane, an Albatros scout. By the end of May he had downed five planes, qualifying as an ace. Though grounded for two months because of an ear operation, he flew back into action in mid-September as Captain and Flight Commander of the famous "Hat-in-the-Ring" squadron. By the end of the war, he had 26 victories to his name, making him the highest US scoring ace – and a national hero when he returned home.

◁ Rickenbacker takes off in one of the fast SPAD fighters issued to the US Air Service in 1918. Ground crew train on the airframes of old Nieuports.

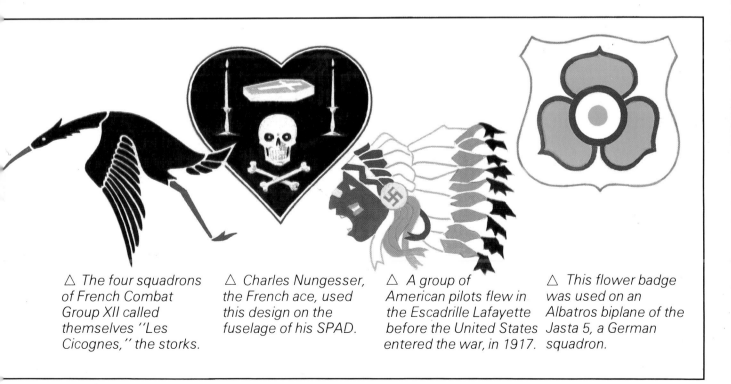

△ The four squadrons of French Combat Group XII called themselves "Les Cicognes," the storks.

△ Charles Nungesser, the French ace, used this design on the fuselage of his SPAD.

△ A group of American pilots flew in the Escadrille Lafayette before the United States entered the war, in 1917.

△ This flower badge was used on an Albatros biplane of the Jasta 5, a German squadron.

Wings over water

Naval air combat was a sideshow to the big air battles over land, although a small but hard-fought struggle took place over the North Sea. Here seaplanes and flying boats fought each other, bombed and torpedoed ships, hunted submarines, spotted targets for big battleships, and intercepted raiding airships and bombers.

One of the most important air bases along the Belgian coast was the German seaplane station at Zeebrugge. It guarded the end of the Bruges canal, used regularly by submarines, and was only 70 km (43 miles) from a big Royal Navy air base at Dunkirk in France.

Zeebrugge's most famous pilot was Freidrich Christiansen. He made 21 kills during his outstanding career, including airships and submarines as well as planes.

In April 1918 he and his unit received the Hansa-Brandenburg W29, a two-seater seaplane that proved to be a superb fighting machine. Two days after a large scale night assault by Royal Navy and Royal Marines on the station, he led a flight of seven W29s which attacked two heavily-armed Allied flying boats. During the long fight, Christiansen attacked from

behind and killed the machine gunner in the rear of one of the flying boats.

Coming alongside, his observer then machine-gunned the oil tank behind the left engine and set it on fire. The flying boat tried to set down on the water but crashed on alighting and burst into flames. On July 6, Christiansen attacked and disabled a diving British submarine, off the coast of Harwich, killing the commander and five crew. Submarine C-25 was credited to his final victory score.

▽ One of the victims of the air war was a British submarine. It was attacked and knocked out by Christiansen in his two-seater W29 seaplane.

He caught the sub on the surface as it was preparing to dive.

A gallant and worthy foe

A pale sun burned through the early morning mist of April 21, 1918, as the Red Baron's new Fokker Triplane lifted off, leading a patrol of five other planes. Sighting two RE8s busily photographing German positions, the Fokkers pounced, but lost their quarry in a bank of cloud.

As the Fokkers disengaged, they were jumped by a flight of Sopwith Camels led by Captain Arthur Brown, a Canadian pilot serving with the RAF.

A novice pilot and fellow Canadian, Lt. May, had his guns jam almost at once and so turned for home. Spotting an easy target, Richthofen gave chase. Brown, in turn, dived after Richthofen.

Hunter and hunted slipped down to a bare 60 m (200 ft) above the Somme valley with the German ace dogging May's desperate zigzagging moves intently – far too intently. Suddenly, Brown had the red Triplane in his sights and fired a burst straight into it.

It looked to Brown as if Richthofen slumped in the cockpit. Nevertheless, the Baron chased May for another half minute at which point May, certain he was doomed, glanced back just in time to see Richthofen half-spin and crash.

A number of Australian troops who had been firing machine guns at the chasing Triplane ran to the wreck. The dead pilot was still at the controls, though it was never certain if the bullet which killed him came from Brown's guns or those of the soldiers. Officially, the victory went to Brown.

A few days later Richthofen's body was buried with full honors. On his grave was laid a wreath from Allied pilots marked "To our gallant and worthy foe."

◁ Captain Brown got the red Triplane in his sights and fired at close range.

The Baron flew on as if nothing had happened. The crash didn't occur until half a minute later, by which time ground troops too had taken pot shots at the aircraft.

Souvenir hunting soldiers stripped the crashed plane, and there was no evidence left as to whose bullet had killed the Baron.

Dogfight!

By 1918, pilots mostly flew in big formations. A single Allied patrol, made up of as many as four or five squadrons, might have had high-flying Snipes, SE5a's at medium height and Camels further down. Each layer provided cover for the fighters below. If such patrols were attacked, huge dogfights would develop, with scores of planes wheeling and dueling anywhere from 7,000 m (20,000 ft) almost down to ground level.

One of the last great dogfights of the war took place on November 4, a week before the war's end, to the south east of Ghent. Two squadrons of Camels at around 3,650 m (12,000 ft) were jumped by some 40 Fokker D.VIIs. In the swirling battle which followed, 22 German planes were knocked out.

One pilot, Captain John White, first destroyed two planes after making tight half-roll turns, coming up from behind to fire fatal bursts of bullets into them. The third he shot down in a cool head-on attack and the fourth he dogged so closely that he forced the Fokker pilot into a vertical spin from which he was unable to recover before crashing.

Massed dogfights of this kind saw all the aerial stunts learned in the previous four years being used. The three most common were spins, half-rolls and climbing turns.

The spin was a dramatic, rotating vertical plunge used to dive out of trouble. The half-roll put a plane into a tight circle on one wingtip, and was the fastest way of turning onto the tail of another plane. The climbing turn was used to gain height over an opponent.

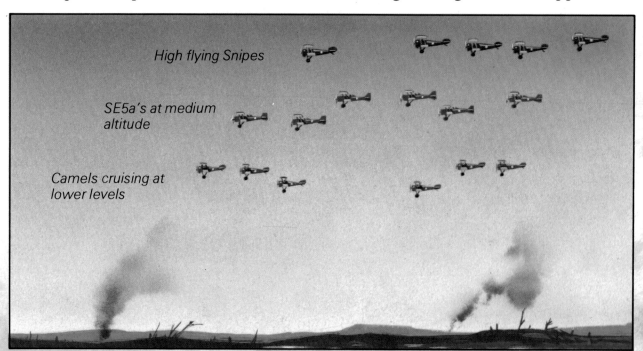

High flying Snipes

SE5a's at medium altitude

Camels cruising at lower levels

Aircraft data

ere are drawings of the main types of aeroplane described in this book. They are drawn to the same scale, so you can compare them in size. These were just a few of the many types that saw action at various times during the war.

▽ **Nieuport 28**
Wingspan: 8.2 m (26 ft 8 in)
Length: 6.4 m (21 ft)
Speed: 196 km/h (122 mph)

▽ **FE2B**
Wingspan: 14.6 m (47 ft 9 in)
Length: 9.8 m (32 ft 3 in)
Speed: 146 km/h (91.5 mph)

◁ **Voisin LA (Type III)**
Wingspan: 15.9 m (52 ft 4 in)
Length: 9.6 m (31 ft 7 in)
Speed: 110 km/h (69 mph)

▽ **RE8**
Wingspan: 13 m (42 ft 7 in)
Length: 8.5 m (27 ft 10 in)
Speed: 157 km/h (98 mph)

△ **Fokker E-III**
Wingspan: 9.5 m (31 ft 2 in)
Length: 7.2 m (23 ft 7 in)
Speed: 140 km/h (87.5 mph)

▽ **Albatros D.III**
Wingspan: 9.05 m (29 ft 8 in)
Length: 7.3 m (24 ft)
Speed: 165 km/h (108 mph)

△ **Sopwith Camel**
Wingspan: 8.5 m (28 ft)
Length: 5.7 m (18 ft 9 in)
Speed: 181 km/h (113 mph)

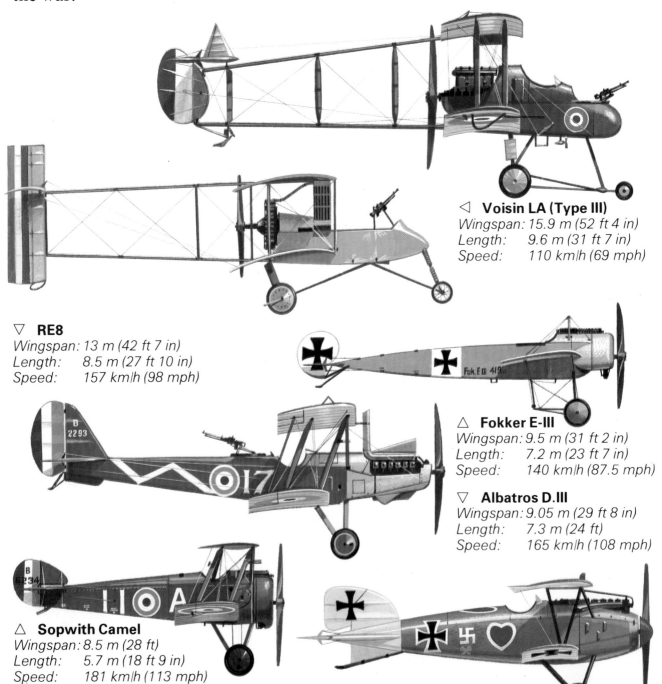

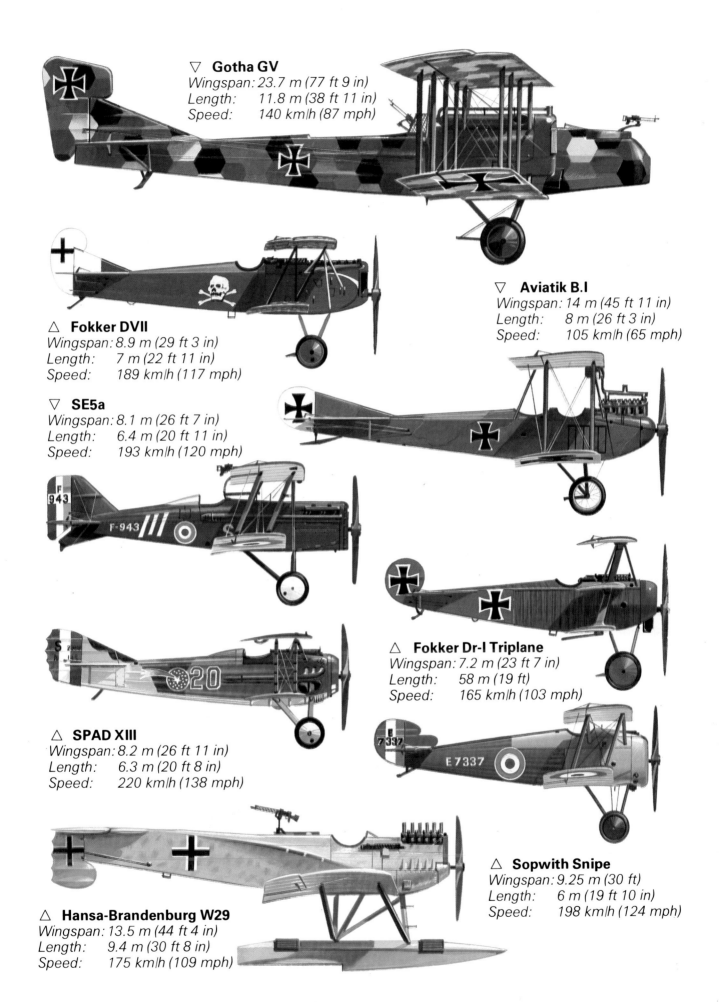

▽ **Gotha GV**
Wingspan: 23.7 m (77 ft 9 in)
Length: 11.8 m (38 ft 11 in)
Speed: 140 km/h (87 mph)

△ **Fokker DVII**
Wingspan: 8.9 m (29 ft 3 in)
Length: 7 m (22 ft 11 in)
Speed: 189 km/h (117 mph)

▽ **SE5a**
Wingspan: 8.1 m (26 ft 7 in)
Length: 6.4 m (20 ft 11 in)
Speed: 193 km/h (120 mph)

▽ **Aviatik B.I**
Wingspan: 14 m (45 ft 11 in)
Length: 8 m (26 ft 3 in)
Speed: 105 km/h (65 mph)

△ **SPAD XIII**
Wingspan: 8.2 m (26 ft 11 in)
Length: 6.3 m (20 ft 8 in)
Speed: 220 km/h (138 mph)

△ **Fokker Dr-I Triplane**
Wingspan: 7.2 m (23 ft 7 in)
Length: 58 m (19 ft)
Speed: 165 km/h (103 mph)

△ **Sopwith Snipe**
Wingspan: 9.25 m (30 ft)
Length: 6 m (19 ft 10 in)
Speed: 198 km/h (124 mph)

△ **Hansa-Brandenburg W29**
Wingspan: 13.5 m (44 ft 4 in)
Length: 9.4 m (30 ft 8 in)
Speed: 175 km/h (109 mph)

The top aces

At the height of the war, the various air services had over 40,000 pilots between them. Of these, a few hundred were skilled enough to be reckoned as aces. Here is a list of the top scorers. The number in front of each pilot's name was his score.

Unconfirmed victories were usually more than this – René Fonck's own estimate was 127, compared to his official total of 75!

Austria-Hungary
40 Godwin Brumowski
32 Julius Arigi
30 Frank Linke-
   Crawford

Brumowski fought mainly against the Italians over the Alps and northern Italy. In 1917, at the age of 28, he commanded groups of up to 18 aircraft.

In late 1917, he and his flyers, including another ace, Linke-Crawford, had control of the Italian skies. But squadrons of Camel fighters were sent from Britain to regain the Allied offensive.

Belgium
37 Willy Coppens
11 André de
   Meelemeester
10 Edmond Thieffry

The Belgian Air Service was small compared with those of the other fighting powers, but it had its share of talented flyers.

Willy Coppens was a balloon buster – of his 37 victories, 26 were balloons. He learned to fly in 1915, when he was 23.

Thieffry was shot down behind the German lines after 10 kills. He was badly injured in the smash, but survived as a prisoner of war.

France
75 René Fonck
54 Georges Guynemer
45 Charles Nungesser

René Fonck was the top-scoring Allied ace. He was 20 when war broke out and on two occasions in the war, shot down six aircraft in one day.

He was a superb shot and used ammunition very sparingly, usually downing an enemy with just a few bullets.

Germany
80 Manfred von
   Richthofen
62 Ernst Udet
53 Erich Loewenhardt
48 Werner Voss

On September 23, 1917, Werner Voss was just two short of 50 victories. That evening, he took off to add the next two aircraft to make his score up to the half century.

It was his turn to be unlucky though – a patrol of Allied aircraft, including one flown by British ace James McCudden, attacked him.

Voss fought brilliantly and put shots in all the opposing planes before the odds overwhelmed him. His Fokker Triplane dived into the ground and exploded. He was killed instantly.

Great Britain
73 Edward Mannock
72 William Bishop
60 Raymond Collishaw
57 James McCudden

In addition to being the top-scoring British pilot, Mick Mannock was a natural flight leader, using his patrols to inflict maximum damage on the enemy.

Billy Bishop was a Canadian, beginning his flying career as an observer in Autumn 1915. He was then just 21 years old. In June 1918, he scored his last victory, leaving for Canada where he helped form the Canadian Air Force.

Italy
34 Francesco Baracca
26 Silvio Scaroni
24 Ruggiero Piccio

Before the war, Baracca was a cavalryman, so he painted a prancing horse on his plane. In 1917, he faced Brumowski's Austrian planes over the Alps. He was shot down in June 1918, but experts thought a ground shot got him, not an Austrian plane.

Russia
17 Alexander Kazakov
15 P.V. d'Argueeff
13 A.P. Seversky

Kazakov had an unusual attack plan. On March 18, 1915 he towed a small anchor behind his plane on a line. On his first attempt, he grappled a German Albatros, then collided with it. He survived, but the enemy crashed.

United States
26 Edward
   Rickenbacker
21 Frank Luke
17 Raoul Lufbery

Raoul Lufbery devised the "Lufbery circle," where a group of planes could fly in a ring, covering each other's tail from enemy aircraft.

Tragically, in May 1918, he died by jumping from his blazing aircraft, rather than face a slow death by fire after his plane was hit by enemy guns.

Glossary

The following terms appear in this book and describe the way aircraft were built, flown and used in battle during World War I.

Ace
A pilot whose score of victories was high enough became known as an ''ace.'' Being called an ace varied according to your nationality. The French and Americans used the term for pilots who shot down five or more enemy planes. The Germans counted from ten or more victories. The British never officially recognized the ace system at all.

Airships
Lighter-than-air balloon with a rigid skeleton that is enveloped by fabric.

Belt-fed
Machine guns whose ammunition is held in long, continuous strips (or belts) rather than in clips or other containers.

Biplane
An aircraft with two wings, one above the other.

Cockpit
Place where the pilot sits and the controls are found by which he flies the plane.

Dogfight
Close combat between two or more planes during which they maneuver to find a position from which their opponent can be shot down.

Field of fire
The arc through which a gun can be swung to give it a clear shot at a target.

Flying boat
An aircraft with a boat-shaped hull that can float, takeoff and land on water. Flying boats were generally far bigger and heavier than seaplanes, which had a pair of floats for landing on.

Fuselage
The body of a plane which houses the engine and crew.

Incendiary ammunition
Shells designed to start fires when they hit a target.

Interrupter gear
Gears to keep a machine gun firing in time with a turning propeller so that the bullets pass between the blades instead of hitting them.

Looping
Flying upward in a circle until a plane flies onto its back, then diving down to complete the circle.

Monoplane
An aircraft with a single wing.

Observation balloon
A lighter than air balloon, with a gondola slung underneath from which observers keep an eye on a large region of battlefield.

Reconnaissance patrols
Flight over enemy lines to observe troop positions, supply dumps, lines of communication and troop movements.

Roundel
The ring-like wing marking with a dot at the center which was used, in various color combinations, to mark Allied planes.

Rudder
Vertical tailpiece on a plane which does the same job as the rudder of a ship.

Shrapnel
Flying fragments of bullets or bombs.

Squadrons
The fighting units into which pilots and planes were grouped.

The Front
The battlefield where opposing lines of German and Allied troops faced each other.

Triplane
An aircraft with three wings, mounted in a stack above each other.

Index

PRINTED IN BELGIUM BY
proost
INTERNATIONAL BOOK PRODUCTION